Stickers for activity on page 27

Stickers for activity on page 15

Stickers for activity on page 34

Stickers for pages 47 and 48

Disney
School Skills

How to Read and Understand

PaRRagon

Bath • New York • Singapore • Hong Kong • Cologne • Delhi
Melbourne • Amsterdam • Johannesburg • Auckland • Shenzhen

This edition published by Parragon in 2010

Parragon
Queen Street House
4 Queen Street
Bath BA1 1HE, UK

ISBN 978-1-4454-1703-5

Printed in China

Dear Parent,

Disney School Skills Workbooks are the perfect tools to make a difference in your child's learning. Inside this book, you'll find a developmental progression of activities designed to help your child master essential skills critical for school success. Interactive stickers help your child learn to read.

Children learn to read at different rates. It takes time and practice. One important part of reading comprehension is background knowledge. In order to make sense of a variety of stories, readers need to have some knowledge about their subjects. Reading every day to your child builds background knowledge. Talking about new words and concepts builds background knowledge. Exposing your child to a variety of life experiences builds background knowledge. It's never too early to start!

Be aware of your child's comfort level. Don't push too much or too little. Make the learning experience challenging yet enjoyable. End on a positive note where your child is eager to pick up a book on his or her own to read more.

As partners in learning with **Disney School Skills Workbooks,** you can help your child reach important milestones to become a confident and independent learner.

Let's Learn to Read

Are you ready for some page-turning fun? This book will give you practice reading real-life and make-believe stories on your own. You'll find stickers and lots more to help you learn to read.

Use your finger to point to words as you read.

Watch where you are going! Read from left-to-right and from top-to-bottom.

Share a book
with a friend.
Talk about parts of
the story you like.

Remember to think
about what you know
to help you read.

Read favourite stories
again and again.

Let's Meet the Princesses

Snow White

Cinderella

Jasmine

Ariel

Belle

Aurora

Let's Read
About Cinderella

Cinderella

Look at Cinderella ride.

Look at Cinderella read.

Look at Cinderella dance.

Look at Cinderella smile!

Let's Understand

Read the questions about *Cinderella*.
Put an ✗ next to the correct answer.

1. The story is about

 ☐ Cinderella

 ☐ Fairy Godmother

2. What does Cinderella do in the story?

 ☐ dance

 ☐ clean

Let's Learn Story Vocabulary

Read the words.
Draw a line to the matching picture.

1. ride

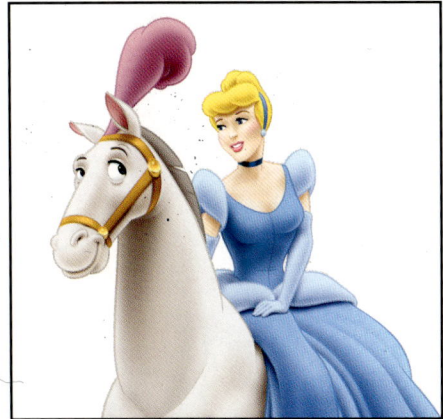

2. read

3. dance

Let's Learn Sight Words

Read the word.
Write the word.

look

_____

_ _ _ _ _ _ _ _ _ _ _ _ _ _

_____

at

_____

_ _ _ _ _ _ _ _ _ _ _ _ _ _

_____

Use a word from the box to complete each sentence.

Look	at

_____

_ _ _ _ _ _ _ _ _ _ _ _ _ _

1. _____ at Cinderella dance.

_____

_ _ _ _ _ _ _ _ _ _ _ _ _ _

2. She is _____ the ball.

10

Let's Learn About Story Characters

Cinderella and Jaq are story characters.
Draw and label one more character from *Cinderella*.

Cinderella

Jaq

_____

_ _

_____

Horses

This is a 🐴 horse.

It has a long tail.

It has four legs.

It is fun to ride.

Colour the tail ✏️.
Colour the legs ✏️.

A Kiss for Dopey

Dopey has a cut on his finger.

Dopey has a cut on his foot.

Dopey has a cut on his head.

Snow White gives Dopey a kiss.

All better!

Let's Understand

Read the questions about *A Kiss for Dopey*.
Put an ✗ next to the correct answer.

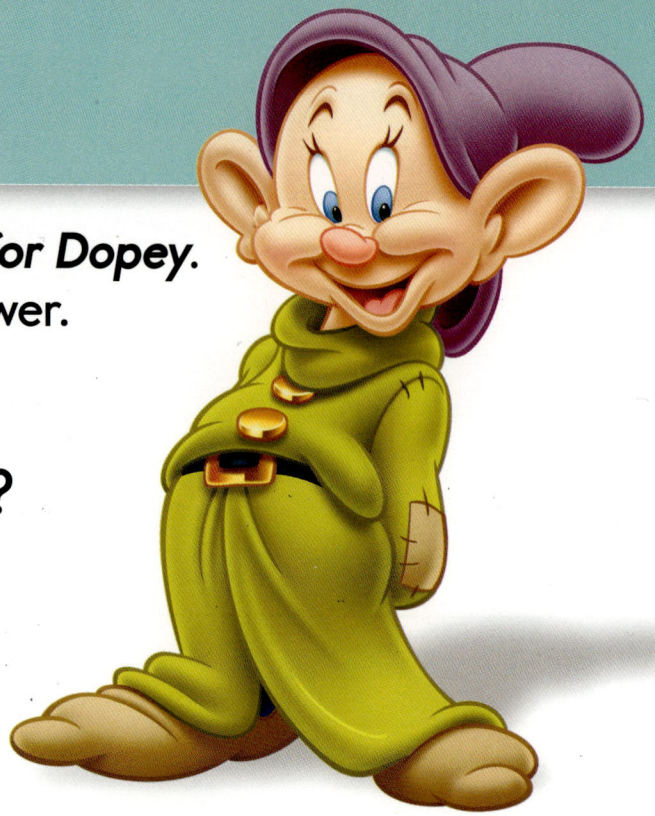

1. What does Dopey have?

   ☐ cuts

   ☐ hats

2. Who helps Dopey?

   ☐ Doc

   ☐ Snow White

3. What makes Dopey feel better?

   ☐ a flower

   ☐ a kiss

Find and match the stickers.
Read the words.
Draw a line to the matching sticker.

1. head

2. foot

3. finger

Let's Learn Sight Words

Read the word.
Write the word.

has

_____

- - - - - - - - - - - - - -

_____

on

_____

- - - - - - - - - - - - - -

_____

his

_____

- - - - - - - - - - - - - -

_____

Use a word from the box to complete each sentence.

his	has	on

1. Dopey _____ a cut.

_____

- - - - - - - - - - - - - -

2. It is _____ his finger.

_____

- - - - - - - - - - - - - -

3. Snow White kisses _____ head.

_____

- - - - - - - - - - - - - -

Let's Learn About Cause and Effect

Draw a picture to complete the chart.
Fill in the missing word.

Dopey is sad

because

He has a _____ .

Let's Learn About Cause and Effect

Draw a picture to complete the chart.
Fill in the missing word.

Dopey is happy

because

Snow White gave him a _____ .

Let's Read About Jasmine

Fly Up High

Jasmine flies up.

Aladdin flies up.

Abu flies up.

Genie flies up.

"I am hungry," says Jasmine.

"Let's eat," says Aladdin.

They all fly down.

Let's Understand

Read the questions about *Fly Up High*.
Put an ✘ next to the correct answer.

1. **What does Jasmine do?**

   ☐ She flies up.

   ☐ She walks up.

   ☐ She stands up.

2. **How does Jasmine feel?**

   ☐ sleepy

   ☐ hungry

   ☐ funny

3. **What will Jasmine do next?**

   ☐ She will cry.

   ☐ She will sing.

   ☐ She will eat.

Read the words.
Draw a line to the matching picture.

1. eat

2. fly

3. down

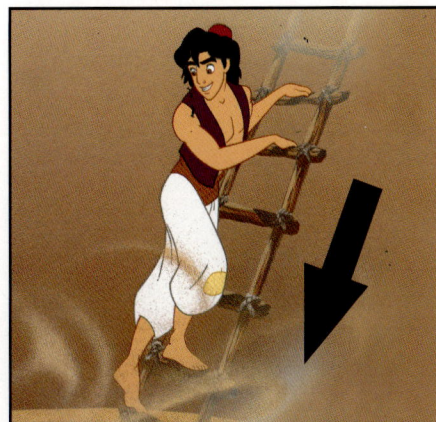

Let's Learn Sight Words

Read the word.
Write the word.

up	I	they
_____	_____	_____
- - - - - - -	- - - - - - -	- - - - - - -
_____	_____	_____

Use a word from the box to complete each sentence.

They	I	up

_____

- - - - - - - - - - - - -

1. Jasmine and Aladdin are _____ high.

"_____

- - - - - - - - - - - - -

2. _____ am hungry," says Jasmine.

_____

- - - - - - - - - - - - -

3. _____ both fly down.

22

Let's Write

Abu likes to eat these foods.

Draw three things you like to eat.

Write a sentence that tells about your pictures.

Food

People eat bananas.

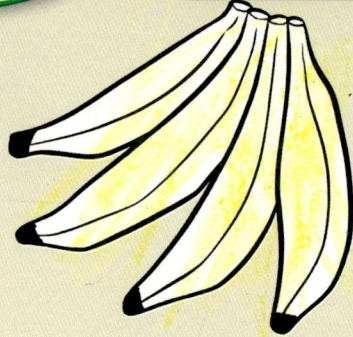

People eat bread.

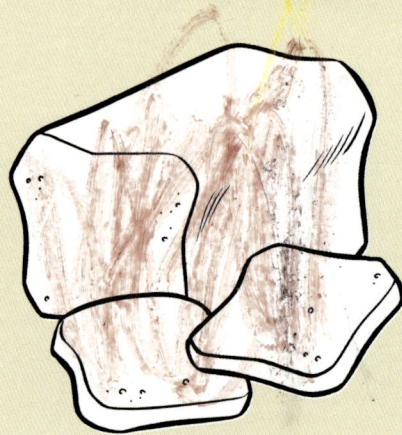

People eat carrots.

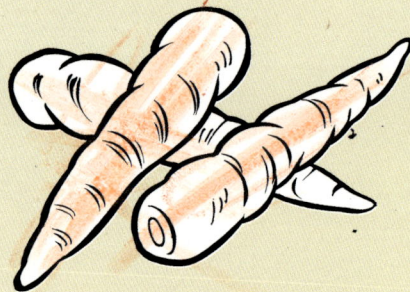

People eat food.

Colour the bananas   .
Colour the bread   .
Colour the carrots   .

Ariel's Friends

Ariel has many friends.

Scuttle can fly.

He is a bird.

Flounder can swim.

He is a fish.

Ariel can swim, too.

She is a mermaid.

Let's Understand

Read the questions about **Ariel's Friends**.
Put an ✗ next to the correct answer.

1. Who is the story about?

   ☐ King Triton

   ☐ Scuttle and Flounder

2. Who is a bird?

   ☐ Scuttle

   ☐ Flounder

3. How is Ariel like Flounder?

   ☐ Ariel can walk.

   ☐ Ariel can swim.

Let's Learn
Story Vocabulary

Find and match the stickers.
Read the words.
Draw a line to the matching sticker.

1. friends

2. bird

3. fish

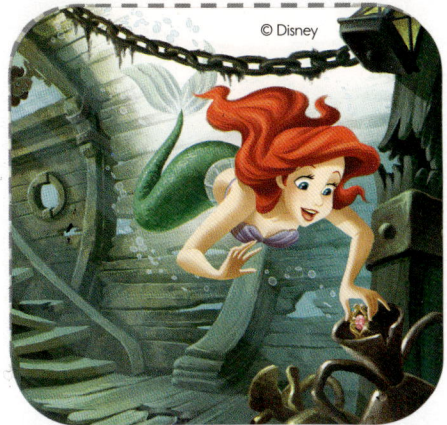

3. swim

Let's Learn Sight Words

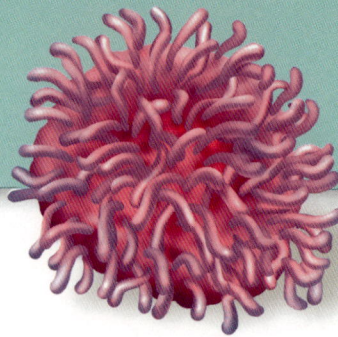

Read the word.
Write the word.

he

_____

- - - - - - - - - - - -

_____

a

_____

- - - - - - - - - - - -

_____

is

_____

- - - - - - - - - - - -

_____

Use a word from the box to complete each sentence.

He   a   is

_____

- - - - - - - - - - - -

1. Scuttle _____ in the air.

_____

- - - - - - - - - - - -

2. Scuttle is _____ bird.

_____

- - - - - - - - - - - -

3. _____ can fly.

28

Let's Write

Ariel finds many things in the sea.

Draw two things you might find in the sea.

Write a sentence that tells about your pictures.

Aurora Gets Ready

Aurora is going to a party.

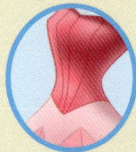

First, she puts on a   dress.

Then, she puts on some   shoes.

Last, she puts on a   crown.

Aurora is ready for the dance!

Let's Learn About Story Sequence

Write 1, 2, 3 or 4 in each ◯
to show what happens in order.

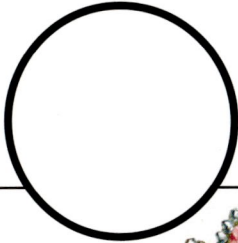

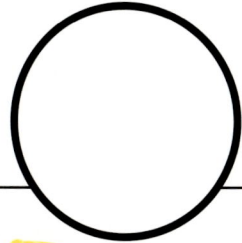

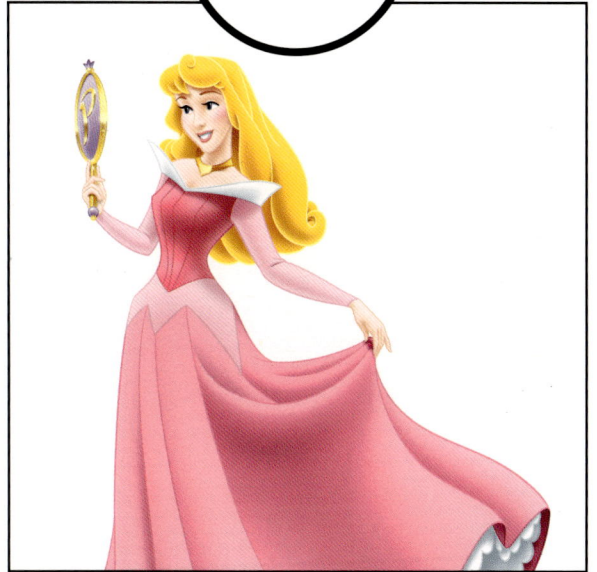

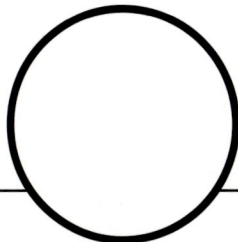

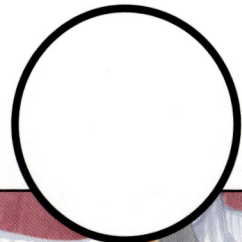

Help Aurora get ready.

Colour the dress ====== .

Colour the shoes ====== .

Colour the crown ====== .

Let's Learn Sight Words

Read the word.
Write the word.

to	then	go
_____	_____	_____
_____	_____	_____

Use a word from the box to complete each sentence.

to	Then	go

_____

1. Aurora will _____ to the party.

_____

2. She will talk _____ the Prince.

_____

3. _____ she will dance.

Let's Read
About Aurora

Read **Aurora's Day**.
Find the stickers on the sticker sheet.
Put the stickers in the right order.

Aurora's Day

First, Aurora wakes up.

Next, Aurora brushes her hair.

Then, Aurora kisses her mother.

Last, Aurora goes outside.

Let's Read

Who Can Fly?

A bird can fly.

A butterfly can fly.

A fairy can fly.

They go up, up, up in the sky.

Draw a picture of something that can fly.

In the Tub

Dirty, muddy tail.

Dirty, muddy toes.

Dirty, muddy back.

Dirty, muddy nose.

In the tub you go!

Scrub-a-dub.

Let's Understand

Read the questions about *In the Tub*.
Put an ✗ next to the correct answer.

1. The puppy is _____ .

   ☐ dirty

   ☐ clean

2. He has mud on his _____ .

   ☐ tail

   ☐ teeth

3. He has mud on his _____ .

   ☐ tummy

   ☐ nose

4. Belle will put him in the _____ .

   ☐ bed

   ☐ tub

Let's Learn
Story Vocabulary

Colour the muddy puppy.
Colour his tail ~~~~~~ .
Colour his toes ~~~~~~ .
Colour his back ~~~~~~ .
Colour his nose ~~~~~~ .

Let's Learn Sight Words

Read the word.
Write the word.

in

you

the

Use a word from the box to complete each sentence.

in	You	the

"_____

1. _____ are dirty!" says Belle.

2. "I will fill _____ bath."

3. "I will put you _____ the bath."

39

Let's Look for Details

Help the puppy get to Belle.

Go to the  .

Go to the 🗝 .

Go to the 🐾 .

Go to 👧 .

FINISH
↑

START ➡

© Disney

Let's Write

Belle likes to dance.

Draw a picture of something you like to do.

Write a sentence that tells about your picture.

Who Am I?

I need a match
To make my glow.
Guess my name.
Give it a go.

I go *tick-tock, tick-tock*.
I bet you know.
Guess my name.
Give it a go.

I pour tea.
Don't you know.
Guess my name.
Give it a go.

Pick me up
By my nose.
Guess my name.
Give it a go.

Answer Keys

Let's Understand

Read the questions about *Cinderella*.
Put an X next to the correct answer.

1. The story is about

   [X] Cinderella

   [ ] Fairy Godmother

2. What does Cinderella do in the story?

   [X] dance

   [ ] clean

Let's Learn
Story Vocabulary

Read the words.
Draw a line to the matching picture.

1. ride
2. read
3. dance

Let's Learn
Sight Words

Read the word.
Write the word.

look   at

look   **at**

Use a word from the box to complete each sentence.

Look	at

1. **Look** at Cinderella dance.

2. She is **at** the ball.

Let's Learn
About Story Characters

Cinderella and Jaq are story characters.
Draw and label one more character from *Cinderella*.

Cinderella   Jaq

Answers will vary.

Let's Read

Horses

This is a ⬤ horse.
It has a long tail.
It has four legs.
It is fun to ride.

Colour the tail.
Colour the legs.

Let's Understand

Read the questions about *A Kiss for Dopey*.
Put an X next to the correct answer.

1. What does Dopey have?

   [X] cuts

   [ ] hats

2. Who helps Dopey?

   [ ] Doc

   [X] Snow White

3. What makes Dopey feel better?

   [ ] a flower

   [X] a kiss

Let's Learn
Story Vocabulary

Find and match the stickers.
Read the words.
Draw a line to the matching sticker.

1. head
2. foot
3. finger

Let's Learn
Sight Words

Read the word.
Write the word.

has   on   his

has   **on**   **his**

Use a word from the box to complete each sentence.

his	has	on

1. Dopey **has** a cut.

2. It is **on** his finger.

3. Snow White kisses **his** head.

Let's Learn
About Cause and Effect

Draw a picture to complete the chart.
Fill in the missing word.

Dopey is sad

because

Answers will vary.

He has a **cut**

Answer Keys

Let's Learn About Cause and Effect

Draw a picture to complete the chart.
Fill in the missing word.

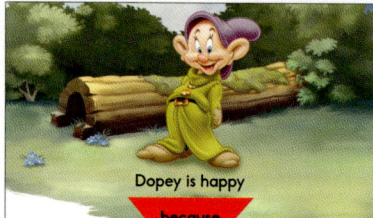

Dopey is happy

because

Answers will vary.

Snow White gave him a _____ **kiss** _____.

Let's Understand

Read the questions about *Fly Up High*.
Put an ✗ next to the correct answer.

1. What does Jasmine do?
   - [X] She flies up.
   - [ ] She walks up.
   - [ ] She stands up.

2. How does Jasmine feel?
   - [ ] sleepy
   - [X] hungry
   - [ ] funny

3. What will Jasmine do next?
   - [ ] She will cry.
   - [ ] She will sing.
   - [X] She will eat.

Let's Learn Story Vocabulary

Read the words.
Draw a line to the matching picture.

1. eat
2. fly
3. down

Let's Learn Sight Words

Read the word.
Write the word.

up — **up**
I — **I**
they — **they**

Use a word from the box to complete each sentence.

They   I   up

1. Jasmine and Aladdin are _____ **up** _____ high.
2. " **I** am hungry," says Jasmine.
3. **They** both fly down.

Let's Write

Abu likes to eat these foods.

Draw three things you like to eat.

Answers will vary.

Write a sentence that tells about your pictures.

Let's Read

Food

People eat bananas.

People eat bread.

People eat carrots.

People eat food.

Colour the bananas
Colour the bread
Colour the carrots

Let's Understand

Read the questions about *Ariel's Friends*.
Put an ✗ next to the correct answer.

1. Who is the story about?
   - [ ] King Triton
   - [X] Scuttle and Flounder

2. Who is a bird?
   - [X] Scuttle
   - [ ] Flounder

3. How is Ariel like Flounder?
   - [ ] Ariel can walk.
   - [X] Ariel can swim.

Let's Learn Story Vocabulary

Find and match the stickers.
Read the words.
Draw a line to the matching sticker.

1. friends
2. bird
3. fish
3. swim

Let's Learn Sight Words

Read the word.
Write the word.

he — **he**
a — **a**
is — **is**

Use a word from the box to complete each sentence.

He   a   is

1. Scuttle _____ **is** _____ in the air.
2. Scuttle is _____ **a** _____ bird.
3. **He** can fly.

Let's Write

Ariel finds many things in the sea.

Draw two things you might find in the sea.

> Answers will vary.

Write a sentence that tells about your pictures.

_____
_____
_____

Let's Learn
About Story Sequence

Write 1, 2, 3, or 4 in each ◯ to show what happens in order.

3 **1**

4 **2**

Let's Learn
Story Vocabulary

Help Aurora get ready.
Colour the dress ____.
Colour the shoes ____.
Colour the crown ____.

Let's Learn
Sight Words

Read the word.
Write the word.

to   then   go

to   **then**   **go**

Use a word from the box to complete each sentence.

| to | Then | go |

1. Aurora will **go** to the party.

2. She will talk **to** the Prince.

3. **Then** she will dance.

Let's Read
About Aurora

Read *Aurora's Day*.
Find the stickers on the sticker sheet.
Put the stickers in the right order.

Aurora's Day

First, Aurora wakes up.

Next, Aurora brushes her hair.

Then, Aurora kisses her mother.

Last, Aurora goes outside.

Let's Read

Who Can Fly?

A bird can fly.

A butterfly can fly.

A fairy can fly.

They go up, up, up in the sky.

Draw a picture of something that can fly.

> Answers will vary.

Let's Understand

Read the questions about *In the Tub*.
Put an ✗ next to the correct answer.

1. The puppy is _____ .
   - [X] dirty
   - [ ] clean

2. He has mud on his _____ .
   - [X] tail
   - [ ] teeth

3. He has mud on his _____ .
   - [ ] tummy
   - [X] nose

4. Belle will put him in the _____ .
   - [ ] bed
   - [X] tub

Let's Learn
Story Vocabulary

Colour the muddy puppy.
Colour his tail ____.
Colour his toes ____.
Colour his back ____.
Colour his nose ____.

Let's Learn
Sight Words

Read the word.
Write the word.

in   you   the

in   **you**   **the**

Use a word from the box to complete each sentence.

| in | You | the |

1. " **You** are dirty!" says Belle.

2. "I will fill **the** bath."

3. "I will put you **in** the bath."

Answer Keys

Let's Look for Details

Help the puppy get to Belle.

Go to the ____.
Go to the ____.
Go to the ____.
Go to ____.

START →
FINISH

Let's Write

Belle likes to dance.

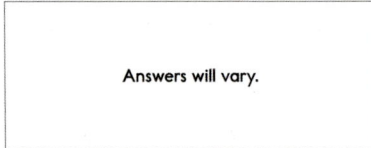

Draw a picture of something you like to do.

Answers will vary.

Write a sentence that tells about your picture.

I can read...

Make-believe stories...

Real-life stories...

Poems...

I can...

Tell about characters in a story...

Tell about a story's setting...

Tell what happens **first**, **next**, and **last** in a story...

Answer questions about stories...

Make connections to my own experiences...

Retell stories...

Name story events that cause other things to happen...

Tell about a story problem and how it was solved...

47

Here are all the things I can do!

You did it! Well done!

I can read story words

back	⬭	friends	⬭
bird	⬭	head	⬭
crown	⬭	nose	⬭
dance	⬭	read	⬭
down	⬭	ride	⬭
dress	⬭	shoes	⬭
eat	⬭	swim	⬭
finger	⬭	tail	⬭
fish	⬭	toes	⬭
fly	⬭		
foot	⬭		

I can read sight words

a	⬭	of	⬭
at	⬭	on	⬭
go	⬭	she	⬭
has	⬭	the	⬭
he	⬭	then	⬭
his	⬭	they	⬭
I	⬭	to	⬭
in	⬭	up	⬭
is	⬭	you	⬭
look	⬭